A souvenir guide

Hardwick Hall
Derbyshire

Bess and the Mans...
4 Early years and hard...
6 Marriage, motherho...
and upward mobility
8 Another convenient
marriage

...er. Bess. A dynasty
is established

The House   14
16 The Great Hall and
Processional Route
18 The State Rooms
20 A room for a queen?
22 Tudor dress code
24 Canopied in splendour
26 Mary Queen of Scots –
The Hardwick legend
28 The family floor
30 A warm welcome
32 Close confines

A House of Treasures   34
36 Carpet that tells a tale
38 The family conservators

Kitchens, Bakery and Buttery   40
42 The ceremony of food

Building Hardwick   44
46 The architecture

The Gardens   48
50 The West Court
52 The South Court
54 The East Court
55 The North Court

The Parkland and Estate   56
58 Improving the prospect
60 The estate today

The National Trust at Hardwick   62

Bess's Legacy   64

National Trust

Bess and the Mansion on the Hill

In the last decade of the 16th century a new mansion, unlike any other, stood on a Derbyshire hilltop. The story of this house and the woman who built it has enthralled generations ever since.

High on a steep escarpment in Derbyshire stands a house of extraordinary presence. The magnificent mansion, testament to the wealth and will of one woman, stands golden on its hilltop. Its west-facing sandstone walls sparkle with fiery light as the setting sun plays across the hundreds of panes of glass.

Hardwick Hall was the marvel of its age. Men and women came to gaze and exclaim at its beauty. The outrageously extravagant glass was even used, in the interests of symmetry, in fake casements covering the stonework.

Towering glory

This prodigy house, completed towards the end of the reign of Elizabeth I, was built by another Bess, a formidable and immensely rich widow. Bess of Hardwick, the Dowager Duchess of Shrewsbury, left no-one in any doubt about the provenance of her new house. She ordered that her initials, E. S., Elizabeth of Shrewsbury, carved in stone and presented underneath her coronet, should stand atop each tower. And there they still are, inviting today's visitors to discover more about Bess, whose story begins and ends at Hardwick. In Hardwick Old Hall, now a ruin, she drew her first breath and in her glittering new house she breathed her last.

Bess's home-coming

In the last years of the 16th century not one but two great houses stood almost side-by-side on top of the hill at Hardwick. One, Hardwick Old Hall, had been renovated and rebuilt extensively while the other, seven years in the making, was ready for occupation.

On a cool morning in early October a procession moved from the old house to the new. Dozens of servants, dressed in smart mallard-blue livery, attended an elderly but sprightly lady and an elegant young woman on the journey, of but a few hundred yards. Some of the retainers played stirring music to mark the long-awaited occasion.

A birthday celebration

In 1597 Bess of Hardwick, accompanied by her 22-year-old granddaughter, Arbella Stuart, at last occupied her new house. Although there was still work to be done, it was fit for habitation. Bess, businesswoman and owner of vast properties, four times married and widowed, mother, step-mother and founder of a great aristocratic dynasty, was coming home to the house whose name would forever be joined with hers.

Above Portrait of Bess of Hardwick, Countess of Shrewsbury, by a follower of Hans Eworth (c.1525–1578)

Opposite The towers of Hardwick Hall and ruins of Hardwick Old Hall

Early years and hard times

Bess was born at Hardwick Hall, then a small manor house, in the mid-1520s. Her father, John Hardwick, a country squire, died when she was less than a year old, leaving his family of five young children in reduced financial circumstances.

The problem was not that there was nothing to leave but, because of revenue-raising rules revived by a cash-strapped Henry VIII, the estate was seized by the Crown and at least half sold into 'wardship'. That meant the family lost control of their land until the heir, Bess's toddler brother James, came of age. The appointed wards could squeeze the revenue from the farms, while Bess's family received nothing. Hardwick Hall and its immediate lands, valued at around £20, remained with the Crown, although the family stayed there, perhaps even paying rent for the privilege.

A step-father for Bess

Bess's mother, also Elizabeth, did the only thing possible to keep her family together; she re-married, becoming the wife of Ralph Leche, the younger son of a Chatsworth family. Ralph owned little but a small annuity of just under £7 a year and income from a few scattered leases. Somehow, even with the addition of three more daughters, step-sisters to Bess, the family managed to survive. Bess, faced with adversity from early childhood, learnt hard lessons that stood her in good stead. For the rest of her life she would fight for what was

rightfully hers, dealing skilfully with financial and legal matters.

She faced her first test when widowed in December 1544, still in her teens, and had to resort to law to receive her widow's 'dower' of one-third of the income from her husband's estate. This was only resolved ten years later, when she was given an annual sum of around £30. It is thought Bess met her young husband, Robert Barlow, in the London household of the Zouch family, distant relatives of the Hardwicks. Bess, as was customary for children of gentle families, was sent to live here, perhaps as companion to the Zouch children. She would have learnt of life at court, how to play music, dance and sew, and was given the chance to read a range of books. Robert, learning to be a courtier, may have been a page.

A child bride

They married, still children, in the spring of 1543. Robert was even younger than Bess and the marriage was unlikely to have been consummated. There is no record of Bess's feelings at Robert's death, but now, a young widow, red-haired and attractive, if not beautiful, she was launched into a world at once brutal and exciting. That world took her close to those at the heart of court life, when it is thought she moved to Bradgate Park in Leicestershire, the home of the ill-fated Grey sisters, Jane, Katherine and Mary. Their mother, Lady Frances, the King's niece, stood fourth in line to the throne. It may have been in this luxurious establishment that Bess met her second husband, the up-and-coming courtier, Sir William Cavendish.

Left This aerial view shows just how close Hardwick Hall and Hardwick Old Hall are to one another

Marriage, motherhood and upward mobility

At Christmastide 1549, Bess, now Lady Cavendish, and Sir William, married for a little more than two years, celebrated the acquisition, for £600, of a parcel of land, including the manor of Chatsworth, in Derbyshire.

Their family already consisted of two daughters, Frances, eighteen months and Temperance who, sadly, was sickly and would not live many more weeks. Bess, just twenty-one, was now mistress of Northaw, the Cavendish manor house in Hertfordshire and their rented house in Newgate Street, London where they entertained extravagantly. She was, by all accounts, a loving and indulgent step-mother to Katheryne and Ann, her husband's surviving daughters by his first wife.

Sir William, married for the third time and more than twenty years older than his new wife, became wealthy during the reign of Henry VIII as a commissioner for the dissolution of the monasteries. Bess persuaded him to sell many of the parcels of monastic land he had acquired and to buy property in Derbyshire. It is significant that the new properties were legally secured in their joint names in such a way that they could never be taken into wardship by the Crown.

S⁺ WILLIAM ÆTATIS · CAVENDISH SVÆ · 44 ·

Right Portrait of Sir William Cavendish aged 44, after John Bettes the Elder (c.1531–c.1570)

Building a life

In two years' time, after the births of two sons, Henry and William, Bess and Sir William embarked on the building of Chatsworth, one of two great houses forever associated with Bess and the great aristocratic dynasty she founded.

But first she learnt the skills of running a great establishment. With the efficiency and energy that she would show throughout her long life, she kept detailed accounts of the rents coming in and the often large sums going out on food and drink, fine fabric for clothes, household goods and wages to servants. She gave generous gifts – a carpet for her sister, small sums to the children and servants who had pleased her, or a hand-out to a poor man who had lost his house in a fire.

A working partnership

It is unlikely that Bess married William for love in the first instance. But she and William had eight children together, six of whom survived to adulthood, and they worked as an efficient team, ensuring their investments in land and property returned the best possible income.

Left This view of Elizabethan Chatsworth by Richard Wilson (1714–82) shows how it might have looked when Bess and William lived there

Below Elizabethan tapestry of Chatsworth

Moving to Chatsworth

By 1555 Bess, and William when he was not required at court, began to live in part of their magnificent new mansion at Chatsworth, still decades from completion. Bess enjoyed overseeing the building work, running the household and learning to keep an eye on the estate. She was able to visit her mother at nearby Hardwick, which would, in time, become the property of her hapless brother James. Did she imagine, at this busy and happy stage of her life that she would one day buy back the old family home and turn it into one of the marvels of the age?

Another convenient marriage

Given the almost twenty-year age gap, it is not surprising that Sir William died before his wife. But the suddenness of his demise, in 1557, by which time Bess had turned thirty, was unexpected.

Her diary records the death of 'my most dear and beloved husband'; in it she asks God 'to rid me and his poor children of our great misery'. She might also have asked the Lord to rid her of the great debt of £5,000 that the asset-rich but cash-poor Sir William owed to the Crown. Bess decided to deal with it in a practical way; she fought the confiscation of her lands and looked for a new husband.

Her six children safely at Chatsworth (her last baby, a girl named Lucres, died soon after Sir William, compounding her grief), she visited London in late 1558 where the Queen, 'Bloody' Mary Tudor lay dying. On her way to and from Chatsworth, it is likely that Bess called in at Hatfield where Princess Elizabeth – godmother to her eldest son, Henry – lived. Bess became friendly with a member of Elizabeth's household, a personable courtier called William St Loe.

The new Lady St Loe

Elizabeth was proclaimed Queen on 17 November 1558. On 26 November, Bess, back in London, sent for her family to join her for Christmas, by which time the Queen had made William St Loe captain of her personal guard, rewarding him well for his service. A month later St Loe's father died, leaving him a wealthy man.

Bess and her second Sir William married in August 1559. The Queen's wedding gift was the appointment of Bess as a Lady of the Privy

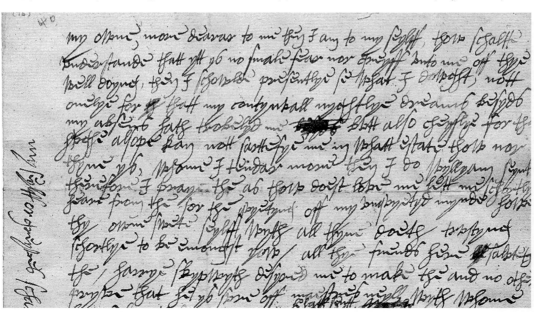

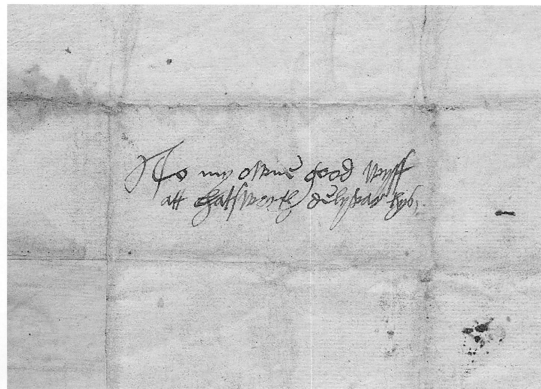

Chamber, so that she became part of Elizabeth's inner circle. Bess's new husband, smitten with his attractive and witty wife, happily accepted her children and step-children, despite the fact that his own two adult daughters from previous marriages must be supported.

'my honest swete chatesworth'

St Loe's letters to Bess show his fondness: 'My own, more dearer to me than I am to myself', begins one. He brings her gifts including furs, gloves, silk, ribbons and velvet shoes and he teases her about her building work which he helps to fund, calling her 'my honest swete chatesworth' and ending another letter referring to her as 'chief overseer of my works'.

Their happiness was short-lived. St Loe died suddenly in London, in February 1565, leaving virtually everything he possessed to 'my entirely beloved wife'. Bess had standing, she possessed significant land holdings and she now had financial security, so that when she returned to court it was not known if she was actively seeking another partner. But when George Talbot, Earl of Shrewsbury, head of one of the richest and noblest families in the country, began to court her in late 1567, she accepted his offer of marriage with alacrity.

Left Detail of a tapestry with rabbits, birds and a village landscape, situated on the Upper Landing at Hardwick

Opposite and above Letters from St Loe to Bess. The one above reads: 'To my owne good wyff att chatsworth delyvar thys'

Love dies and Bess begins to build

The spectacular rows during the final years of Bess and George Shrewsbury's marriage reverberate through the centuries, but their trust, affection and even love were evident at the beginning.

They were well-matched in intellect and ambition. Shrewsbury's early letters to her begin 'My sweet None' (a corruption of 'mine own') or 'My own dear Heart'. But the enormous burden, placed on them by the Queen of guarding Mary, Queen of Scots for long years, took its toll on the marriage, costing more than even the wealthy Earl would countenance.

Some historians believe that Shrewsbury became afflicted with a form of dementia, causing him to mistrust everyone, including Bess. His violent action, in summer 1584, forcing her out of her own house, Chatsworth, and claiming it as his, spurred his fugitive wife to take on her last great building project. In 1583 Bess had bought her old family home from the estate of her brother James who died, bankrupt,

in Fleet prison. She packed up the silver plate, items of furniture and valuable textiles and fled to Hardwick when Chatsworth, along with Shrewsbury's other houses, was barred to her. Once settled she did what she'd always done – called in the builders and began to turn Hardwick Old Hall into a grand mansion.

From tragedy to triumph

Bess, in her sixties, was as full of energy and ambition as ever. Although she fought her case against her husband, she wasted no time in turning her misfortune into a triumph. Soon she had transformed her childhood home, with the addition of two enormous wings, each containing a grand 'great chamber'. Here stood a huge two-storied hall, built, unusually, in the centre of the house and there was glass – a lot of glass.

Right George Talbot, 6th Earl of Shrewsbury. This striking portrait is either a later copy of a lost original, or an 18th-century pastiche based on a known head-and-shoulders portrait from 1580

Opposite The now ruined Hardwick Old Hall, which Bess remodelled in the 1580s

Opposite right Lady Arbella Stuart, aged 23 months, holding a doll that bears more than a passing resemblance to Elizabeth I. The painter is unknown

The lofty state rooms at the very top of the house were lit by these windows. But Bess was not going to stop there. Hardwick Old Hall, occupied by Bess, her son William and his family and her grand-daughter, Arbella Stuart, in the throes of completion, she began to oversee the digging of the foundations for her last and greatest project.

Rising from the ashes

Hardwick Hall, gloriously designed, radically conceived and undeniably modern, rose from the ashes of her marriage. Bess's estranged husband died in November 1590, just as the new house that would proclaim her name, wealth and status from its rooftops, was begun. The leading building designer of the day, Robert Smythson, almost certainly drew the initial layout, but there is no doubt that much of this extraordinary Elizabethan mansion sprang from the mind of Bess herself.

After Bess: A dynasty is established

When Bess died, in her early eighties, in 1608, she left Hardwick, along with the furniture from Chatsworth, to her favourite son, William.

She could not leave him Chatsworth, which was entailed on her eldest 'bad son' Henry, but it became William's in 1609 when Henry, deeply in debt, sold it for £8,000. The staggering sum of £10,000, paid to the Crown in 1618, saw William become Earl of Devonshire. Bess,

hugely ambitious for her children, would have been delighted and more so in 1694, when William's great-grandson was created the first Duke of Devonshire, establishing the dynasty that flourishes today.

William made Hardwick his principal home, entertaining the Prince of Wales, the future Charles I, here in August 1619 and spending considerable amounts on refurbishment. His hapless son, William 'Wylkyn' lived only two years longer than his father but managed to

Above Hardwick Hall's West Court with its majestic cedar planted by Lady Blanche Howard in 1832

spend much of the family fortune. Wylkyn's Scottish widow, Christian Bruce steered the finances back on track and was responsible for setting up the then fashionable canopies in the High Great Chamber and Long Gallery.

A mansion in mothballs

Thereafter Chatsworth became the main residence of the Cavendish family, while Hardwick was carefully preserved as a perfect Tudor house. The house chose its caretakers well. Four members of the family, in particular, loved Hardwick. The 6th 'Bachelor' Duke, William George Spencer Cavendish, born in 1790 and known as 'Hart', inherited at least eight stately homes. But he valued Hardwick most. He wrote in 1844 to his sister Harriet that it was here that their mother, the unhappy Georgiana, Duchess of Devonshire, spent 'the happy part of a harassed life'. Conscious of the unique nature of the tapestries and embroideries, many made by Bess herself, he began to catalogue and look after them. The Bachelor Duke died at Hardwick in 1858.

Above right Lady Blanche Howard, Duchess of Devonshire, after John Lucas (1807–1874)

Right William Spencer Cavendish, the Bachelor Duke, by an unknown painter

Hardwick's remarkable women

The Bachelor Duke's niece, Lady Blanche Howard, married his successor. She died at the age of twenty-eight, in 1840, before her husband inherited. 'She passed some of the happy months of her short life here,' wrote the Bachelor Duke, who credited her with making the flower garden during the summers she spent here. Lady Howard, with head gardener George Holmes, created astonishing carpet bedding in the West Court and oversaw the planting, in 1832, of two tiny cedars, one of which is now a 'champion' tree.

Blanche died when her daughter, Louisa, was a small child. Like her mother Lady Louisa was a passionate gardener, devising the division of the large South Court with a clever mix of yew and hornbeam hedges. Later she made her hand-written 'Notes and Alterations' with sketches, cataloguing the collection of Hardwick. The last of the remarkable women of Hardwick who devoted themselves to its care was the Dowager Duchess Evelyn. Until the National Trust took over in 1959, the cultured and knowledgeable Duchess undertook the restoration of Hardwick's irreplaceable embroideries and tapestries, ensuring a priceless legacy to generations of visitors.

The House

Modesty is not a feature of this house. Bess decreed that her initials and coronet should crown the parapets in fourteen places. Glass, the most expensive of all Elizabethan building materials, proclaimed her wealth.

Today's visitors approach Hardwick Hall through the gatehouse that guards the West Court. A wide flagstone path, flanked by well-kept lawns, leads to the entrance. Above are those towering windows, expanses of glittering glass. Higher still, standing between two of the six great turrets emblazoned with Bess's initials, is her coat of arms incorporating the Hardwick stags with their collars of wild roses or eglantines. The scene is as impressive today as at the end of the 16th century.

Seeking a lost past

But Bess, summoned back across four centuries, would have marched around in bewilderment, listening for the bustle and noise of maids and manservants running to and from the stableyard with its dairy, brewhouse, bakehouse, smokehouse and slaughterhouse and cobbled stalls filled with restless horses.

What had happened to her sheep-filled orchards and beehives and apple stores? Where was the little hay meadow and why

Opposite One of the two stags (with real antlers) on the house front, which support the Hardwick coat of arms

Above The striking gatehouse with its elaborate finials and decoration

Below right Bess's coronet and initials stand out clearly on each of the towers

couldn't she hear the rumble of oxen-drawn carts and wagons bringing goods to both her houses? And, above all, what had happened to Hardwick Old Hall, home to her son William and as much part of her domain as the new home which still appears, from the outside, much as it was when she was head of the grand household here? The ghost of Bess would remember these two households, run together and sharing a complement of more than seventy servants.

Self-sufficient households

Both Hardwick households would have shared milk, cheese, cream and butter from the dairy, fish from the stewponds, meat from cattle grown fat on estate land and slaughtered and butchered in the Stableyard.

There were herds of deer in the park for sport and supper, and fruit in the orchards. The henhouses, filled with fowl looking more like game birds than today's domestic hens, would produce eggs and provide meat for the kitchen. The sheep that grazed the orchards would be shorn and their fleeces spun to make garments while honey for sweetening food and beeswax for the hundreds of candles used in both houses

would be taken from the beehives in due season. The bees meanwhile ensured good fruit crops as they busily worked the blossom of dozens of apple, plum and pear trees in the orchards. Teams of carpenters, stonemasons, farriers and other workmen made the place ring with the noise of their tools and busy chatter.

When we walk through the door into Hardwick Hall today, let's try to enter as visitors from the early 17th century and see the scene through their eyes.

The Great Hall and Processional Route

Our visitors, dressed in their finest clothes, had been anticipating this first invitation to Hardwick Hall with excitement, but as they spotted the sculpted initials and massive coronets displaying the credentials of its formidable owner, literally from the rooftop, they perhaps became a little nervous.

The house, smaller than expected, was nevertheless as beautiful and spectacular as they had heard. Perhaps, as they walked underneath the massive coat of arms and up to the entrance, they glanced up to wonder how many pairs of eyes watched from those enormous windows.

Servants above stairs

Elizabethan servants did not live 'below stairs' but within calling distance of their master or mistress. At Hardwick the 'upper servants' – usually the sons and daughters of good families learning to be courtiers – lived in Hardwick Old Hall. The 'lower servants' did the hard jobs, including the cleaning, cooking and scullery work. Their 'common room' was the Great Hall. At night they slept on straw mattresses on landings, in the kitchens, outside bedrooms in the Great Hall or in one of the turrets.

Right The Great Hall, with its stone screen of pure classical style dating from 1597

Opposite Prominent over the chimneypiece is a plasterwork overmantel of the Hardwick coat of arms

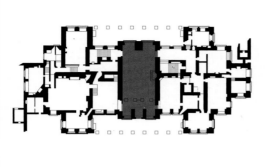

The Hall today
The brightly coloured Hall tapestries of Bess's day could have been the 'Devonshire Hunting Tapestries' (above), now in the Victoria and Albert Museum. The tapestries shown today represents *Scenes of County Life and Proverbs*. On the wall facing her coat of arms is a portrait of Bess in her early fifties. The antlers, crowning the armorial stags' heads are real – added by Lady Louisa Egerton in the 19th century.

They would not have been surprised, as they stepped through the heavy wooden door into the Great Hall, to be assailed by a barrage of noise and bright colour. The loud chattering of dozens of servants, eating, playing cards or simply gossiping, suddenly subsides as the usher, striding forward to meet these new guests, shouted over the noise, calling 'Pray silence, my masters!' Our visitors stepped forward to a low murmuring as the blue-liveried servants, called to order, clustered together, watching their progress through the great room. As they made their way past three long highly polished tables, gleaming in the candle-light from the wall sconces, they glanced at each other to acknowledge sight of Bess of Hardwick's coat of arms again, finely worked in plaster, in prime position over the fireplace.

Dazzled by fabric

No newcomer to Hardwick could ignore the bright furnishings. Our guests would have stopped to admire the dazzling colours of the tapestries, which seemed to cover every inch of the walls. Woven in deepest crimson, scarlets, bright blues and greens, they showed people and animals in a forest setting.

As they were escorted to the far end of the Hall, to embark on the long walk to the top of the house to meet their hostess, they glanced back towards the entrance, admiring the finely carved stone screen supporting a gallery that appears to connect rooms on the first floor. They paused again, gesturing and talking quietly to each other as they realised that this Hall is aligned like no other they have entered before. Instead of lying across the width of the house it is placed exactly in the centre, running from front to back.

The State Rooms

At last our visitors were escorted from the Hall and ushered to the foot of a wide flight of shallow stone stairs curving gently upwards.

From the kitchens, somewhere to the left, wafted the smell of roasting meat. Light from a great glass lantern flickered on the bare white-washed walls. The spiralling steps reached a half-landing where a closed door was guarded by the carved head of a sentry, his forbidding features topped

by a flaming grenade – a warning that this door, leading to family rooms, is out of bounds.

Bess's guests had heard that when she re-fashioned Hardwick Old Hall she broke with tradition by building her grandest rooms on the upper floors. She carried this idea across to her new house, sandwiching the less formal family rooms in the middle. Nevertheless, these stairs seemed endless as the way ahead narrowed and curved out of sight. The couple paused to catch their breath on the next landing where stood a table covered by a rare and precious Turkish carpet, an Oushak rug, one of many at Hardwick. Carpets, too precious to use as floor coverings, decorated tables or chests.

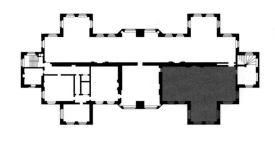

The High Great Chamber

Upwards once more, until, finally, they reached a light-filled landing. They glanced at each other as a servant bowed and threw open the door to a room so vast, they could not help gasping before making a dignified entrance. The other guests were already assembled. A long table, covered in a damask cloth was prepared for dinner. Ahead, their hostess, the dowager Countess of Shrewsbury, sat in her elaborately embroidered chair with its gold and silk fringe, waiting to receive them. The company seemed lost in this wide space, offset by the glowing colours of the extraordinary frieze emblazoned around the upper half of the wall. Above the chimneypiece they noticed the arms of the Queen, Elizabeth I. Brussels tapestries covered the lower walls, telling the story of Ulysses and his patient and faithful wife, Penelope. Prominent too was a showy looking-glass decorated with the royal arms, while impressive brass fire dogs guarded the fireplace.

Opposite Bess and her honoured guests would have climbed these broad stairs in stately procession to reach the High Great Chamber

Above Close-up of the frieze in the High Great Chamber

The eglantine table

Today light from the windows illuminates the ancient 'eglantine' table, probably made to celebrate the triple marriage in 1567 of Bess to George Talbot, the Earl of Shrewsbury, and her two children, Henry and Mary Cavendish, to his daughter and son, Grace and Gilbert Talbot. Entwined Cavendish, Talbot and Hardwick arms are beautifully inlaid, as are board games, musical instruments and sheet music, including the four-part motet *Oh Lord in Thee is all my Trust*. The collar of eglantines, or sweetbriar, worn by the stags is part of the Hardwick family crest.

A room for a queen?

Bess knew that Queen Elizabeth, now an old lady, would never travel to Hardwick. So today we ask why this high-ceilinged suite of rooms on the top floor was built to rival those in a royal palace?

The answer may lie with Bess's granddaughter, Arbella Stuart, whose father, Charles Stuart, a direct descendant of Henry VII, married Elizabeth Cavendish, Bess's second daughter. Arbella's claim to the English throne was as good (and some thought better) than that of her cousin, James, who succeeded Elizabeth in 1603.

The Long Gallery

Back to our Tudor visitors, who, relaxed after enjoying the food that had been carried ceremoniously through the Hall, would have retired with the other guests to the Withdrawing Chamber or perhaps the Long Gallery.

Those guests, unprepared for the sheer size of the Long Gallery, would have found this room just as marvellous as the High Great Chamber. In Bess's day the main decoration was a series of brightly coloured tapestries. There were few pictures; Bess mentions 37 small portraits in her will, two inlaid tables, again covered with priceless carpets, embroidered window seats and a few chairs, stools and forms.

The thirteen large Flemish tapestries showing Gideon defeating the heathen Midianites were

Above The Long Gallery at Hardwick is the largest surviving Elizabethan long gallery and the only one to retain its original tapestries and many of its original pictures

Right The view of the Long Gallery from the north alcove towards its stunning alabaster chimneypiece

---

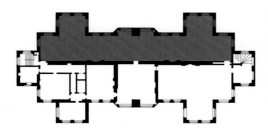

Arbella's story

There is no doubt that Bess and Arbella's other grandmother, Margaret Douglas, Dowager Countess of Lennox, contrived to bring their children, Elizabeth and Charles, together. When the young couple married without royal permission, Margaret was punished by an angry Queen Elizabeth with a spell in the Tower, while it seems Bess got off lightly with a severe dressing down. Arbella, just six when her mother, Elizabeth Stuart, died in 1582, was brought up by Bess who fondly referred to her, and all her other grandchildren, as 'my jewel'.

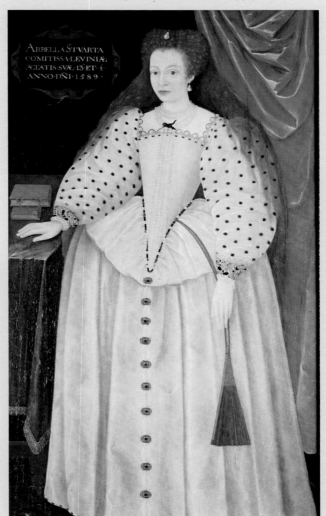

bought by Bess in 1592 for £326 15s 9d from the estate of Sir Christopher Hatton, once Queen Elizabeth's Lord Chancellor. They were made for his palatial Holdenby House, but sold after his death in 1591 to help pay debts. Sharp-eyed visitors today will notice that pieces of cloth bearing Bess's arms cover the Hatton shields, while Sir Christopher's heraldic does have been turned into Hardwick stags by the addition of painted antlers and eglantine collars. Astute Bess reduced the asking price of the tapestries by £5 to cover the cost of this work.

Tudor dress code

We will leave Bess's guests crowded round the full-length portrait of Queen Elizabeth, now at the far end of the Long Gallery.

The painting, thought to have been made in the workshop of miniaturist Nicholas Hilliard, was hanging at Hardwick in Bess's day. The decorations on the Queen's extraordinary dress would have been 'decoded' by the assembled company.

A wake-up call

The 6th 'Bachelor' Duke loved the effect the Long Gallery had on tired visitors: 'People begin to get weary and think they have done, and to want their luncheon; but they are awakened when the tapestry…is lifted up and they find themselves in this stupendous and original apartment.' He probably did not disclose to those visitors that, as a young man, he used to race his greyhounds down the length of the room. The servants were often called to mop up after the excitable dogs.

The iris must symbolise Her Majesty's much-lauded virginity, while the pearls signify purity and the snake, wisdom. She is holding her gloves (representing love) against the Chair of State which stands for England, thus she must love her realm. And she is standing on a carpet, a privilege afforded only to the richest and most powerful. Most of today's pictures, many covering the tapestries, were arranged in clusters by the 6th Duke in the first half of the 19th century.

Above This watercolour by David Cox (1783–1859) show what the Long Gallery would have looked like in the 6th Duke's time

Left Portrait of Queen Elizabeth, from the studio of Nicholas Hilliard

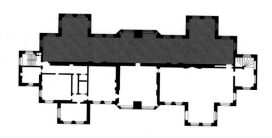

Below This portrait of Bess, probably by Rowland Lockey (c.1565–1616), which hangs in the Long Gallery, shows her as a tough old widow in black in about 1600

Portraits of the builder

In the Gallery today are two portraits of Bess, the earlier made in about 1560. Red-haired Bess wears a fashionable black, mink-lined gown, decorated with gold 'aiglets' or fastenings. She has pearls over her collar and on her French hood, gold bracelets and four gold rings on her slim fingers. The later painting, a version of her last known portrait, is dated about 1600. Here an older and gaunt Bess wears widow's black. Arbella's portrait is here too, showing a wide-eyed girl of sixteen, wearing pearls – probably her grandmother's – and a white satin gown, elaborately trimmed with gold and black.

Arbella's story

In early January 1603, Bess and her granddaughter, Arbella, were walking in the Long Gallery when Royal Commissioner, Sir Henry Brounker, arrived with a message from the Queen. He was gentle with Bess but insisted that he must speak alone with Arbella. Arbella Stuart was intelligent and well-educated. Bess loved her, but was unable to find her a husband.

Elizabeth insisted that, because of Arbella's royal blood, any marriage must be sanctioned by the Crown. So the young woman, feeling imprisoned at Hardwick, had plotted to marry young Edward Seymour – another descendant of Henry Tudor. Her plan uncovered, Sir Henry was despatched from Court to get to the bottom of her machinations.

Bess, heartbroken, the more so after a botched attempt in early March by Arbella to escape from Hardwick, begged that Arbella be 'placed elsewhere'. But no-one was listening. All attention was focused on Richmond, where the sick Queen had taken to her bed. In the early hours of 24 March, Queen Elizabeth died and Arbella's cousin, King James of Scotland, succeeded to the English throne.

Canopied in splendour

In early Tudor days magnificent 'cloths of state' overhanging chairs or thrones were reserved for royalty, but 17th-century aristocrats began to copy the idea.

Christian Bruce, wife of the 2nd Earl, installed the High Great Chamber canopy before it was moved to Chatsworth by the Bachelor Duke, who thought it 'too glaring' for Hardwick. It was reinstated by the National Trust in the 1990s.

The Long Gallery canopy, fashioned from a magnificently upholstered bed, made for the State Bedroom at Chatsworth, was brought here by the Bachelor Duke, conscious of its theatrical impact in this already dramatic chamber.

1 The Withdrawing Chamber
Today the room that Bess reserved for entertaining her favourite visitors has lost some of its grandeur, with the 18th-century lowering of its once lofty ceiling. Her select gatherings would have enjoyed musical entertainment, card games, or simply conversation and a nightcap. Here is the walnut 'sea-dog' table, which may have been given to Bess by Queen Elizabeth or Mary, Queen of Scots. The fine scroll-work on this once-gilded table and the quality of the carved

Bess goes shopping
At the end of 1591 Bess, Arbella and a large portion of their household moved to London for nine months, where Bess embarked on a massive spending spree, buying clothes, gloves, shoes, fabrics, jewels, silver and gold plate and furnishings, including the Hatton tapestries (see page 21), for her new house. When she returned home in July 1592 her meticulously kept accounts show she had spent a staggering £6,360.

Left The canopy in the Long Gallery is a magnificent example of late 17th-century upholstery

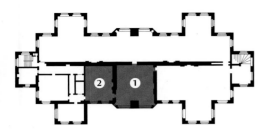

chimeras or sea dogs with their acanthus-leaf ears, women's breasts and dolphins' tails, suggest it was made for royalty. Other Elizabethan pieces include carved cupboards and a square games table, inlaid with a board, listed in Bess's inventory of 1601. A colourful marquetry chest bearing the initials GT was the wedding chest of Mary Cavendish, Bess's youngest daughter, and Gilbert Talbot. At bedtime the most important guests would retire next door, to the Best Bedchamber, now the Green Velvet Room.

2 The Green Velvet Bedroom

Although the Bachelor Duke abhorred the alabaster and blackstone surrounds to the door and chimneypiece, it was he who installed the magnificent bed which came, with its green velvet hangings and matching chairs, from another Devonshire family house, Londesborough Hall in Yorkshire. The carved gilt stools were from Chatsworth. The 'Abraham' tapestries were bought, like the Gideon set in the Long Gallery, from the estate of Sir Christopher Hatton in 1592. They were stored as a spare set which explains their fresh and comparatively unfaded colour.

Top right Two-tier cabinet in the Withdrawing Chamber

Right Supported by chimeras or sea-dogs resting on tortoises, the walnut table in the Withdrawing Chamber is one of the most important pieces of 16th-century furniture in England

Mary, Queen of Scots – The Hardwick legend

In early 1567 Bess married her fourth husband, the immensely rich George Talbot, Earl of Shrewsbury.

The country squire's daughter could now claim the coronet of a countess. She brought her Cavendish and St Loe lands to the marriage, while Talbot offered not only his main home, Sheffield Castle, but several great houses and acres of land. Bess retained lifetime rights over Chatsworth House and rental income from some Talbot properties.

A poisoned chalice

Within a year of their marriage, Shrewsbury was handed what appeared to be a great honour. The Queen charged him with guarding Mary, Queen of Scots. He and Bess, initially delighted at the trust Elizabeth had placed in them, came to realise the constraints and massive expense this custodianship involved. They could no longer split their time between

A great cover-up

Rush matting covered the state room floors from the late 16th century. It gradually fell out of use but was re-introduced by Duchess Evelyn. Hardwick lends its name to this matting, which must be watered to keep it supple.

Right This portrait of Mary, Queen of Scots hangs in the Long Gallery

Below The Mary, Queen of Scots Room

Right Over the door of Mary's room is this panel enclosing the Scottish royal arms and the initials MR (Mary Regina)

Chatsworth and Sheffield Castle. Bess sat with Mary, sewing, embroidering and making new gowns. But these companionable sessions were disrupted as Mary was moved between properties, such as dismal Tutbury, adding to the expense and tensions between the Shrewsburys. By the time Mary was executed at Fotheringay Castle in 1587, the Shrewsburys were leading separate lives.

1 Room of legend

Why is there a chamber at Hardwick bearing the name of a queen who was executed before the house was built? The legend that she had lived here grew over the centuries, so it seems the chamber was furnished to feed the myth. In Bess's day this room was part of an apartment – the Little Chamber within the Best Bedchamber. Now it is suitably dramatic, with Mary's arms (probably brought from Chatsworth, where she had been sometime imprisoned) over the door and black lacquer furniture matching the black velvet bed. A portrait of Mary with her husband, Lord Darnley, who was murdered in 1567, two years after their marriage, hangs close by.

2 The Blue Room

When Bess was married to William Cavendish they splashed out on thirteen great beds, many embroidered with silver, gold and pearls, for Chatsworth. The Blue Room at Hardwick contained such a bed in Bess's day, when it was known as the Pearl Bedchamber. Today's beautiful blue bed is a copy of one belonging to Christian Bruce, wife of the 2nd Earl of Devonshire, and bears her arms.

The Brussels tapestries, showing gods and planets, were listed in Hardwick's 1601 inventory, while the figures on the overmantel tell the story of Tobias and the Angel – a story Bess enjoyed, owning as she did, tapestries and a table carpet also relating to the tale.

The family floor

The North Staircase, each step a single piece of oak, leads down to the first floor, where the house seems to breathe more easily and become less formal.

The grand scale of the suite of state rooms on the second floor, from the great windows, the size of the chambers and the height of the ceilings, was designed to impress. This family floor is still grand but more comfortable and on a less intimidating scale.

Above The Cut-Velvet Bedroom

Opposite The Cut-Velvet Dressing Room

1 The Cut-Velvet Dressing Room and Bedroom

The 1601 inventory lists these two rooms as the Tobies Chamber and the Ship Bedchamber. At that time the Tobit tapestries (see pages 36–7) were hanging in the smaller room. When William Cavendish became the first Duke in 1694, he not only rebuilt Chatsworth, but also altered this floor to create apartments for himself and his Duchess, Mary. The Brussels tapestries in the Cut-Velvet Bedroom, telling the story of the prodigal son and of the mother-goddess Cybele, are contemporary with the house, while the overmantel bears not only Bess's arms, but also her initials linked with those of her second husband, William Cavendish.

2 The Low Great Chamber

Bess, her relatives and her close friends used this room for their gatherings. It was a real family room, furnished for eating at one long table and with two smaller square tables for playing games and cards. There were embroidered chairs and stools, made comfortable with cushions, for relaxing and reading.

Later generations used it as a family dining room. The furniture, mainly late 18th-century mahogany, was collected by the Dowager

Duchess Evelyn who liked this light chamber better than 'the over-decorated dining room at Chatsworth'. Both she and the 6th Duke made good use of the large window bay. Duchess Evelyn would bring tapestries and needlework here to be repaired in the good light. More than one hundred years earlier, the 6th Duke, then a boy, confined his menagerie of rabbits, hedgehogs, guinea pigs, white mice and even some sad birds, perching on an imported tree, to this deep recess. Accounts recall the 'melancholy hooting' of an owl – and an overpowering smell.

There is an oval portrait of the 6th Duke, hanging with his Cavendish relatives, on the south wall of this room.

Tudor family fun

We know, not only from her accounts, but also from a letter written by her son, William Cavendish, that Bess loved entertaining. He wrote that in his mother's home 'holidays' were occasions for fun and games. 'All the old holidays with their mirth and rites…May games, Morris dances, the Lord of the May, the Lady of the May, the Fool and the Hobby Horse, also the Whitsun Lord and Lady, carols and wassails at Christmas, with good plum porridge and pies…'

Right These pink and green cut-velvet hangings were made in about 1740 by Thomas Vardy

A warm welcome

Bess's personal 'Withdrawing Chamber' in the eyes of today's visitors, is the most welcoming room in the house. It was used until 1959 by the Dowager Duchess Evelyn, the last family member to live at Hardwick.

Evelyn welcomed her guests with a comfortable mix of 16th-century tapestries and needlework panels (some possibly embroidered by Bess herself), deep armchairs and warm rugs on top of Hardwick matting.

The tapestries were bought by Bess, during her 1592 shopping spree, from Sir Christopher Hatton's estate, as were the 'Gideon' tapestries upstairs. Hatton's arms on the hangings were covered by 'my Ladies Armes', says the 1601 survey, but the cloth-painted Hardwick arms have been removed from five of the pieces.

The blue and white china collection in the 18th-century Dutch cabinet includes a Ming porcelain jug which could have been at Hardwick from early days; its silver-gilt mount is dated 1589.

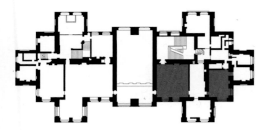

Re-covering the chairs

The 18th-century chairs around the cabinet were 'discovered' by Lady Louisa Egerton and her daughters. Lady Louisa's great-niece, Maud Baillie, wrote of the 'excitement' when Victorian chintz covers were removed to reveal a 'barely decipherable…beautiful design in silk and wool needlework. The best draughtswoman among the daughters set to work to reproduce this design and the whole set of chairs was eventually re-covered, some by my mother [the Duchess Evelyn] and grandmother.'

Portraits include Henry VIII and his son, Edward VI. The ill-fated couple, Mary, Queen of Scots and her husband, Lord Darnley, are here too, as is Arbella Stuart, painted when she was almost two years old. The chubby youngster, holding a doll, gazes out, unaware of the heartbreak ahead.

Bess's herbal

A passageway leads to the bedchamber used by Bess and, later, by the 6th Duke. Its last occupant was the Dowager Duchess Evelyn. Octagonal needlework panels copying designs from 16th-century botanical plates are displayed in the passage. The 32 canvas-work pieces, depicting plants and herbs bordered with mottos, are thought to have been part of the Best Bed hangings, which are recorded in the 1601 inventory.

Bess's Bedroom

This room, the private bedchamber of Bess, ended up as the bedchamber of Dowager Duchess Evelyn, who lived at Hardwick Hall until 1960, devoting herself to the conservation of its contents, especially the tapestries and other needlework. Three-hundred-and-sixty years earlier, Arbella Stuart, a grown woman in her early twenties, shared this room with her seventy-year-old grandmother. Arbella slept under 'a canopy of darnix blue and white with gilt knobs and a blue and white fringe', while Bess's bed was laden with coverlets for warmth in this chilly house. The room, larger then, was part of the family suite shared by Bess, her son William and Arbella.

Opposite above
The Drawing Room

Opposite below **Ming** dynasty porcelain jug with Elizabethan silver-gilt mounts

Below Three of the octagonal canvas-work panels in the Drawing Room Passage, based on a engravings in a contemporary herbal

Close confines

Bess's four-poster bed was surrounded by scarlet curtains, made of wool, matching the colour of those over the windows.

There were warm rugs on the floor, coverlets and extra hangings for the windows in very cold weather. Her writing desk with its

tethering-ring, perhaps for a little dog, was in here too. A small room next door housed 'close stools' or commodes for Bess and Arbella. Bess's granddaughter had her own study, but because it had to be reached through Bess's suite of rooms it was, felt Arbella, 'a disadvantageous chamber'.

The route to the ground floor takes you across the galleried landing, where you can view the Hall from above, and into the Paved Room, intended as a landing, but at one time used as a dining room for the upper servants and later as a bedroom.

Left The rare painted wall-hangings in the Chapel depict the life of St Paul

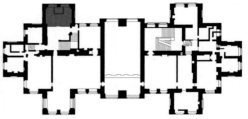

Virtuous women

On the landing are displayed Zenobia with Magnanimity and Prudence, and Artemisia flanked by Piety and Constancy, two of the four rare and important 'Virtuous Women' hangings in the Hardwick Collection.

Arbella's story

When Queen Elizabeth died in 1603, Arbella left Hardwick to join the court of the new king, her cousin James. By 1605, when she was thirty, it was clear that James would not allow her to marry. She would be the suspected focus of a plot to overthrow the sovereign. In 1611, three years after Bess's death, she secretly married William Seymour, twelve years her junior and, like her, of royal descent. They were apprehended within days and imprisoned, he in the Tower and she under house arrest. Arbella, with her grandmother's mettle, plotted their separate escapes and, disguised as a man, rode to Blackwall on the Thames where she was to meet William. She had arranged a barque to take them across the Channel to freedom. William successfully escaped, but missed the tide. By the time he set sail from Harwich, Arbella's boat, caught just off the Calais coast, by the English ship *Adventure*, had been boarded and Arbella arrested. She was taken to London and locked in the Tower. No-one bothered to search for her husband who landed at Ostend and spent the next four years abroad. Arbella died in the Tower of London, it seems from self-inflicted starvation, in September 1615.

Above **The Chapel**

The Chapel

This was the upper gallery of the chapel, used by family only, while the servants worshipped on the ground floor. That lower area was converted to a steward's room by the 5th Duke. The wall-hangings, painted with scenes from the life of St Paul, are rare survivals of what was once a common alternative to tapestry. It is thought that John Ballechouse ('John Painter') made them at the turn of the 16th century. In 1601 three pictures of the Virgin and an embroidery of the Crucifixion hung in the Upper Chapel.

A House of Treasures

Hardwick's collection of Tudor and Stuart needlework is renowned worldwide. The house is unique in that much of its original furnishing is still in place.

Opposite Penelope, symbol of patience and faithfulness in Greek mythology

Left The Fancie of a Fowler, 16th-century cushion cover

Flemish tapestries, carpets from Persia and Turkey, rare painted wall-hangings, embroidered cushion covers and bed-hangings are displayed throughout the house and in the exhibition rooms on the ground floor.

Rare and precious hangings

You'll find treasures such as the 'Virtuous Women' hangings, made from sumptuous materials cut from ecclesiastical copes (cloaks). Silks, satins, cloth of gold and velvets have been stitched together to show Penelope, Lucretia, Zenobia and Artemesia. These are some of the most important Elizabethan needlework pieces in existence. The large panel showing Penelope, flanked by her 'virtues', Patience and Perseverance, is shown in the 'Stitches in Time' exhibition on the ground floor. It is lit to give some idea of its original glowing colours and luxurious materials. Penelope, the patient and faithful wife of Ulysses, waits twenty years for her husband to return from the Trojan wars, refusing to re-marry or take a lover. Her delaying tactic is the burial shroud she must finish weaving before she will consider another relationship. She secretly unpicks the work and is eventually rewarded by the return of her adventurous husband.

Original material

A series of rooms display Hardwick's treasures and describe the history of the house. In 1601, when Bess was making her will, she undertook a survey of the contents. Many of the items listed in this detailed inventory are shown today. These include the finely worked cushion cover, 'The Fancie of a Fowler', thought to have been made to celebrate the marriage of Bess's son, William Cavendish, to Anne Keighley in 1581. The initials 'AC' and Anne Keighley's family arms are shown hanging from a tree above the pastoral scene.

Stitches in time

Much of the work was made for Bess's Chatsworth and brought to furnish Hardwick in the 1590s. Bess always employed at least one 'imbroderer', her accounts showing that he was given rooms in Hardwick Old Hall in 1591. The inventory shows that 'beames for imbroiderers' were kept in the New Hall. These 'beames' would have been the frames on which pieces such as cushion covers were worked. Bess was a fine needlewoman and, working with her gentlewomen, would have made many of the smaller pieces.

A material source

Bess's second husband, William Cavendish, worked for Henry VIII's chief minister, Thomas Cromwell, as a commissioner for the dissolution of the monasteries. He 'acquired' a store of church property, including the beautiful vestments from which some of the pieces at Hardwick were made. More copes came from her third husband, William St Loe.

Carpet that tells a tale

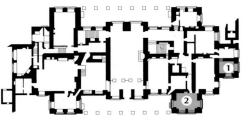

We know that Bess used carpets for warmth in her own bedchamber and that full-length portraits of the very rich and important would show the subject standing on a carpet. But carpets were usually ornamental, covering tables or chests.

The magnificent Tobit carpet is, effectively, an embroidered table cover, made for Bess and her husband George Talbot, the Earl of Shrewsbury in 1579. Scenes from the story of Tobias and the Angel (see panel) are shown on

Tobias and the Angel
This was a popular story in the 15th and 16th centuries, when the angel Raphael was seen as a protector of travellers. There is a full set of tapestries and an overmantel telling the tale at Hardwick, as well as the glorious carpet. Briefly, Tobias, son of blind Tobit, sets out on a long journey from Nineveh to Media, accompanied by a 'guide' who, unknown to Tobias, is the angel Raphael. He catches a magic fish on the way. In Medea his host's daughter, the beautiful Sarah, is possessed by a devil who kills any man she takes as husband. Tobias falls for Sarah and, on Raphael's advice, he burns the entrails of the fish to destroy the devil and the couple are wed. Not only that – a salve made from the fish cures his father's blindness when the happy couple and their angel finally arrive home.

this beautifully restored piece, embroidered in coloured silk floss on a thick linen cloth. At the centre is the date, 1579, and the Hardwick arms and entwined Cavendish, Shrewsbury and Talbot initials.

1 The Muniment Room

This small room, all four walls filled from floor to ceiling with 17th-century drawers, once housed all the documents and title deeds (or muniments) relating to the Cavendish estates. The documents were filed here from 1603 although the drawers (each numbered to make searching easier) weren't installed until the mid-17th century. The little room next door is known as the Evidence Room where stewards would sit to read the documents.

2 The Duke's Room

The 8th Duke, a quiet man who stayed at Hardwick every autumn for the shooting, made a 'den' for himself in this tucked-away room, which he furnished with a red carpet and sofa and chairs. When Bess lived at Hardwick this was probably the room occupied by her favourite half-sister Jane Leche. Jane, who became Mrs Knyveton, lived with Bess from 1548 as a lady-in-waiting, earning 15 shillings each quarter day.

Left Detail of the Tobit carpet

The family conservators

Many of Hardwick's original furnishings, some bought especially for the house by Bess and others moved from Chatsworth, were cared for by later family members who regarded their Elizabethan house with affection.

One of the first to conserve the furnishings, in particular the tapestries, was the 6th Duke, a great collector and art lover. He brought the tapestries showing the tragic story of Hero and Leander from Chatsworth to hang along the first flight of stairs and covered hitherto bare walls with others. He grouped family portraits and pictures in the Long Gallery, hanging them, as today, over tapestries, and brought the 'Virtuous Women' hangings from two of the bedrooms to stand together in the High Great Chamber. The Duke, when at Hardwick, used Bess's bedroom, and it was here he died in 1858.

Working for Hardwick

His great-niece, Lady Louisa Egerton, who kept house for her widowed father, the 7th Duke, was deeply attached to Hardwick. Her brother, Spencer Compton, who inherited the title, lent her the house for several months each year. Her great-niece, Maud Baillie, remembered Louisa and her daughters devoting their 'whole time and energy' working for Hardwick. They repaired needlework, cleaned plasterwork and explored the turrets, discovering long-forgotten objects.

Louisa's handwritten 'Notes and Alterations' detail the excitement in 1901 when pieces of the 'spare tapestry' were spread about the Long Gallery floor in an attempt to fit them together. These, 'cut and pieced together incorrectly with heads and bodies separated without reference to sex or subject' had been correctly identified by a visitor as rare 15th-century French tapestries. Eventually assembled into the four Devonshire Hunting Tapestries, they are now displayed at the Victoria and Albert Museum. The 1601 survey indicates that two of these tapestries hung in Bess's bedroom, while four more were displayed in the Entrance Hall.

A labour of love

Louisa's duty of care was handed to Duchess Evelyn whose husband inherited in 1908. Hardwick became her dower house when her Duke died in 1938, from which time she devoted herself to restoring the needlework and tapestries. A fine needlewoman, she did much of the work herself, experimenting with cleaning methods and undertaking the 'infinitely laborious' process of weaving with a needle to repair the tapestries.

A-hunting we will go
Duchess Evelyn's daughter, Maud Baillie, remembered another jigsaw puzzle session with the 'Verdure' tapestry, now hanging on the main staircase landing. It had, she wrote, been 'ruthlessly cut' to fill gaps. She, her sisters and mother assembled 25 pieces, missing only the brush of a fox. Maud spent hours on hands and knees tacking the pieces together when the odd job man 'appeared one day with the joyful news that he had found the missing fox's brush in a dark corner'. Duchess Evelyn 'worked the joins together till they were almost indistinguishable from the original weave'. The Duchess later wrote: 'I think this is the pleasantest of tapestries to live with.'

Left Evelyn Fitzmaurice,
Duchess of Devonshire
by Edward Irvine
Halliday (1950)

Kitchens, Bakery and Buttery

Hardwick's turrets, a distance away from the ground floor kitchens, were used not only as bedrooms and, in one case, a banqueting room, but also to store cooking equipment.

Bess's great inventory lists dozens of pewter items tucked away in a turret. These included dishes, saucers, porringers, bowls, flower pots and chamber pots and other necessaries, such as 15 kettles, skimmers, spits, a beef fork, mortars and pestles, frying pans, chopping knives and gridirons. Presumably these were spare items, as the climb upstairs would have been time-consuming for a cook looking for a frying pan while rustling up dinner.

The ground floor, with the exception of the Great Hall, which rises through two storeys, is low-ceilinged. There were bedrooms and nurseries here, but to the north of the Great Hall were the service rooms: the kitchen itself, the 'pastry' (the bakery, where bread was made daily), the scullery and the pantry, used for storing baked food, table linen and the table silver. Cellars below the pantry held casks of beer and wine. The buttery, where the beer was poured, later the Butler's Pantry, lies to the south of the Hall.

Hot and dangerous work

Baking was done in brick-lined ovens while everything else was cooked over huge open fires, using spits, pans, kettles and trivets. It was hot and often dangerous work. The Kitchen today reflects the time of the 6th Duke; the solid furniture was installed in the late 18th or early 19th century. His funeral hatchment, displayed on the outside of the house when he died here in 1858, hangs on the wall.

Underneath the window is a rare late 17th-century 'stewing hearth' which was gradually developed into the more recognisable cast-iron closed oven range. The Elizabethan Serving Room displays records giving some insight into the lives of Hardwick servants.

Left Looking into the Kitchen

Right The cast-iron range in the Kitchen

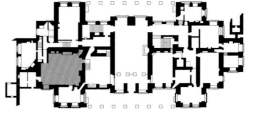

Quince cakes with a view

Today a banquet means a great feast. In Elizabethan times it was the last, or sweetmeat, course taken while the dining chamber (the High Great Chamber or the Low Great Chamber at Hardwick) was being 'voided' or cleared for after-dinner entertainment. Bess liked to take her guests across the 'leads' of the roof to the south turret, or banqueting room, where they could admire the view and enjoy quince cakes, jellies and creams, marmalade biscuits, candied fruits and Banbury cake. There was another such chamber on the ground floor and two in the garden.

The ceremony of food

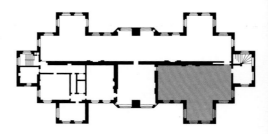

Bess, used to life at court, ran her own household on the same lines. Her inner circle consisted of her family and her gentlewomen.

Her son William lived across the garden in Hardwick Old Hall, although his children were taught in the ground-floor schoolroom of the new house. Her granddaughter Arbella Stuart and her ladies-in-waiting helped entertain guests, provided companionship and worked with her on the embroideries for which Hardwick is famous.

Water works

There was no running water at Hardwick at the beginning of the 17th century. It was pumped from a well to a lead cistern in a brick building to the south of the Hall before being piped to cisterns in the kitchen. Sanitation was primitive. There were latrine shafts at Hardwick Old Hall (although these privies may have been built after Bess's time). In the Hardwick Hall bedrooms were provided with 'close-stools' and chamber pots.

Time to eat

Breakfast was generally taken early, between six and seven o'clock. Fine white 'manchet' loaves, spread with butter, and perhaps some fruit or a sweet pancake would be served with a mug of 'small-beer'. Everyone avoided drinking water unless certain of its source, so mead or weak ale, sometimes spiced with nutmeg or mace was drunk instead. Dinner, served between 11 and 12 in the morning, was an elaborate affair. Bess liked to entertain in style. Each of her Hardwick houses had two 'presence chambers' (the High Great Chamber and the Forest Great Chamber in Hardwick Old Hall) where she would offer guests splendid dinners and entertainment.

Dining in style

As the company seated themselves around the long white wooden table, covered with damask cloths and decorated with an elaborate centrepiece, the food, borne on silver platters and embellished with peacock feathers, cloth of gold or colourful fruits, would be carried around and handed to each guest. Diners picked up their knives and sliced morsels on to their plates. Sometimes dozens of dishes would be offered, carried from the kitchens, up the great staircase, the sumptuous procession saluted by all who met it. The first course could have included venison pasties, minced salmon in a mustard and vinegar

Above *The Banquet of Monarchs*, by Alonso Sanchez Coello (*c*.1590) in the National Museum, Warsaw, vividly depicts the elaborate splendour of Elizabethan banquets

sauce, humble pie (made of deer offal), goose in sorrel sauce, roast lamb, swan, capon or pigeon. Saucers – dishes with dipping sauces – were placed within reach of each guest. Bones, gristle, pips and peel were thrown into 'voiders' to be removed by the servants.

After a short break there would be another, even more elaborate course with more fish and meat dishes, but also tarts of custard and pears, jellies and baked fruits. Ale and wines were served before guests rose to partake of

sweetmeats in the 'banqueting room' (see page 41). Supper, another main meal but a less elaborate affair, was served between five and six in the evening.

Building Hardwick

Bess was over sixty when she embarked on building the house that was to survive virtually unchanged for more than four centuries after her death.

She had had plenty of practice, devoting more than thirty years to building Chatsworth House, which, although since redesigned, remains the main home of the dynasty she founded. She knew what she wanted in her homes. She liked to build high, enjoying the flourish of towers or turrets. She liked her grandest rooms on the top floor and she demanded symmetry, which was ruthlessly achieved at her new house at Hardwick by covering walls with huge expanses of expensive glass.

Robert Smythson

We will never know how much of an input the fêted master mason of the day, Robert Smythson, had in the design of Hardwick. Bess certainly knew him. He had remodelled Worksop Manor for her estranged husband, the Earl of Shrewsbury, and was involved in the design of her friend John Thynne's beautiful house at Longleat. We know that Bess paid a small amount to Smythson and his son in 1597, the year she moved into her new home. It is likely that he provided some ideas, or plans and elevations, while she, with her team of master masons, did the rest.

It is also likely that she learnt from her experience of rebuilding her old family home, the now-ruined Hardwick Old Hall. It was grand, tall, with many windows and lofty rooms at the top of the house. It had turrets and possessed two enormous Presence Chambers, but it lacked elegance and symmetry. The haphazard nature of the Old Hall, built in a hurry and still being worked on as the foundations for her latest home were dug, may have made her think carefully about the appearance of her new house.

Left As the Hall faces west, its façade catches the setting sun

Bess's army of builders

A small army of men (and some women) worked on the building. They included masons, wallers, paviours, carpenters, lathmakers, sawyers and slaters, plasterers, plumbers, glaziers, smiths, painters, mat-makers and embroiderers. A few women were paid 1d a day to help the men making the plaster and mortar. Materials for the house, including sandstone and limestone, the lead, glass, alabaster, timber and Derbyshire blackstone, were locally sourced. Bess owned many of the coal mines and quarries surrounding Hardwick, and men from her mines provided some of the labour.

Above Hardwick Hall has always been known for its shimmering walls of glass

Stonemasons

Stonemasons still work at Hardwick today, using stone from the park that yielded the ashlar blocks used for the house over 400 years ago. Each mason has his own mark, a device of a few lines in a unique pattern. This was, and still is, used to show which craftsmen made a particular piece of work. Almost 50 different marks have been identified at Hardwick Hall.

The architecture

Hardwick espoused Elizabethan ideals of symmetry but used a radical interior design to achieve perfection.

Medieval and early Tudor tradition dictated that the Great Hall should lie along the entrance front, but here it has been turned ninety degrees, so that it is exactly central, running from front to back through two storeys. On either side of the Hall the building takes the shape of two matching Greek crosses. At the top of the house the 'arms' of these crosses at roof level form the base of the six turrets, which are the crowning glory of Hardwick. On the

A winning team

Three craftsmen in particular – plasterer Abraham Smith, stone carver Thomas Accres and painter John Ballechouse – were responsible for much of the interior decoration. Master mason Accres not only carved the marble and alabaster fireplace surrounds, but also devised a machine for sawing the local 'blackstone'. Bess was so delighted that she not only paid his 10 shilling bill, but also gave his wife 20 shillings to buy a gown 'in respect of her husband's device in sawing blackstone'. The High Great Chamber frieze was likely to have been made by Abraham Smith and his team and coloured by John Ballechouse. Bess employed these three men on a long-term basis, giving them rent-free farms and paying them generous bonuses.

west, or entrance, front the space between the turrets is emphasised by a colonnade. The same decoration is used on the east side.

A built-in device

The turrets themselves, a feature Bess had used at Chatsworth and Hardwick Old Hall, fulfilled another Elizabethan ideal – that there should be some mystery, some 'device' built into everyday objects. These towers are symmetrical, but they form an ever-changing pattern as you walk around the building, their grouping appearing to move through each turn.

We learn from her accounts that Bess's new house took roughly seven years to build. Her teams of labourers and craftsmen, still working on the old house, were with her for the long-haul. Twenty men dug the foundations and cellars in late 1590, covering the courses in straw over the winter to prevent freezing. The labourers were fed, paid 4d a day and slept under a lean-to of hurdles. The ground floor was built in 1591, the family floor the following year, while the second floor was completed in 1593. In 1594 the roof and turrets were built. The paving and glazing were completed in early 1597. By the end of that year the decoration, interior and exterior was almost complete and Bess was able to move in.

Right Hardwick Hall's stately grandeur, its vast expanses of window glass and the great height of its six towers make it one of the most perfect of all Elizabethan 'prodigy houses'

The Gardens

Early letters from Bess show that she felt a garden was an essential part of any home.

In March 1560, long before the prospect of a house at Hardwick, Bess, recently married to Sir William St Loe, was enjoying herself at Court, but thinking about her new garden back at Chatsworth, already occupied by her family but still in the hands of the builders. Letters flowed back and forth between Bess and James Crompe, the steward looking after her estates and overseeing the building work. With the arrival of spring, Bess began to plan the garden.

She wanted her mother's sister to take charge of it, writing to Crompe: 'I would have you tell my Aunt Linnacre that I would have the new garden which is by the new house, made a garden this year. I care not whether she bestow any great cost thereof, but to sow it with all kinds of herbs and flowers, and some piece with mallows. I have sent you by this carrier three bundles of garden seeds…from the Court this 8th March.'

Above Purple-flowered cardoons and hops reach great heights in the Herb Garden

Courtyard gardens

Although we have no record of how the gardens were arranged when Bess returned to Hardwick, we know that they lay in the four rectangular walled courtyards that she planned in the last decade of the 16th century. She would have ensured, first of all, a sustainable herb garden, serving both households. It is likely that she would have grown flowers there too – probably lavender, wallflowers (gillyflowers), primroses, cowslips, columbines, violets, wild honeysuckle, heartsease (pansies), roses and garden pinks. She would have planted orchards and a hay meadow for winter fodder for any animals kept over winter. Sheep might have been kept in the orchard – mutton and wool providing food and fabric.

Productive and pretty

Bess would have known from her upbringing exactly what a Tudor household needed from its garden. It had to work for its keep, providing plenty of herbs, not only for flavouring food and drinks, but also for medicines. There were apples for cooking and eating and varieties of small crab apples which were made into jellies for winter use. Medlars were another valuable winter fruit. Cherries, gooseberries, damsons and pears were grown for dessert. Some salad vegetables, once viewed with suspicion, were now eaten regularly by the rich, using any combination of chervil, rampion, lettuce, garlic, fennel, sage, parsley, cucumber, kale, borage, mint and watercress, dressed with seasoning and oil and vinegar, much as today. Onions and leeks, cabbages, carrots, parsnips and pumpkins had become known and acceptable by the end of Elizabeth's reign.

Above right Cotton lavender edges the paths in the Herb Garden

Far right Sweet peas are grown for scent and colour

The West Court

Bess's walled courtyards frame the house today. Each is roughly rectangular and designed to match the facade that it faces. In total the courtyards, those to the north and south much larger than the other two, encompass roughly 7 hectares (18 acres) of gardens, set within wider parkland.

After Bess's death and the removal of the family to Chatsworth, little was done to develop the gardens apart from desultory attempts to keep the weeds in check and mow the grass until, in 1660, 'old John Booth' arrived from nearby Edensor with his rake, hoe and spade and was paid £1.1s 10d to make a kitchen garden with the help of a few labourers and a local housewife, who pulled the weeds.

Lady Blanche's design

The Elizabethan garden had disappeared by the beginning of the 19th century, although the walls still defined its space, then a member of the family took the planting in hand. Lady Blanche Howard, niece of the 6th Duke, stayed here often. In 1832, when she was the young wife of William Cavendish (later the 7th Duke), she started work on the West Court. She began by planting two small cedars of Lebanon, grown from seed and nurtured in small pots in the greenhouse. One, now a magnificent 'champion' tree, shades a corner of the Court. The other, damaged by gales and snow, was removed in 1991.

Blanche, in tribute to Bess, devised an elaborate bedding-out plan with a mix of plants creating the letters 'E and S' (Elizabeth Shrewsbury) flanking either side of the pathway. Her gardener, George Holmes, carried out the scheme, using pelargoniums, lobelia, marigolds and daisies. The surrounding borders, planted with dark-coloured azaleas, rhododendrons, dahlias and carnations with a border of standard roses alongside the path, made a striking design which was maintained until 1920, when it was turfed over. Poor Blanche was just 28 when she died in 1840, but her love of the garden was inherited by her daughter, Louisa.

Today the West Court has magnificent mixed borders running the length of the walls. Designed in 1985 by the then Gardens Advisor to the National Trust, they were planted over the next few years by the Hardwick gardening team. The colours and heights of the often rare plants are graded dark to light, with taller specimens nearest Hardwick Hall to add perspective and frame the house to its best advantage.

Opposite This 19th-century photograph shows the parterre garden with Bess's initials (Elizabeth Shrewsbury)

Left The north-facing herbaceous border in the West Court

The South Court

Left The rondell, where paths meet and sculptures inhabit alcoves cut into the yew hedges

Above The Ornamental Orchard

Opposite Hardwick's Herb Garden is one of the best in the country

This large area linked Bess's two households and contained the herb and vegetable gardens, orchards and paddocks that served them both. It led to the Stableyard that was also used by both Hardwick Hall and Hardwick Old Hall.

We don't know the layout in Tudor and Stuart times, but today the South Court retains the shape devised by another of the women who helped make Hardwick what it is today. Lady Louisa Egerton, Blanche Howard's daughter, was barely more than a toddler when Blanche died. When she grew up, she enthusiastically continued her mother's work of 40 years earlier. Before her marriage to Admiral the Hon Francis Egerton, Louisa helped 'keep house' for her widowed father, who became the 7th Duke in 1858. Offered Hardwick as her summer home, she set to work on the South Court, with the help of Edmund Wilson, head gardener from 1872 to 1925.

Defining the courts

In the second half of the 19th century, she turned what was a large empty paddock into four equal compartments with grass walks defined by hornbeam hedges running from east to west and yew hedges on the north-south axis. The walks meet in a central rondell of yew into which domed alcoves have been cut to contain 18th-century lead statues, brought from Chatsworth.

Culinary and medicinal herbs

In the south-west segment is the spectacular Herb Garden, one of the largest in the country, planted early this century. Designed by Isabelle van Groeningen in 2004, it has been developed from a structure created by the Trust in the mid-1970s. Here are at least 150 varieties of culinary and medicinal herbs, many of which would have been known and used by Bess. Flowers grown to decorate the Hall have their own border, while vegetables for use in the restaurant flourish here too. The adjoining Nuttery is planted with two varieties of cobnut, one unknown, the other, growing in the shade of the large walnut tree, 'Nottingham Prolific'. The remaining quarter, the South Lawn, possibly the original kitchen garden for Hardwick Old Hall, was once used as a tennis court. This area, now grassed, contains fine specimen trees.

These compartments provide the framework for today's gardens in the South Court. Here you'll find the Ornamental and Fruiting Orchards. The former contains species crab apples. Paths are mown through its grassy underskirt, which is planted with cowslips and spring and early summer bulbs. The Fruiting Orchard contains old varieties of apple and different types of pear, plum, damsons and greengages. A stunning autumn show of dahlias shines from a border in this area.

Smoking shelter?

The mulberry walk leads to a garden gazebo, a small sandstone building in the corner of the Court, where, on fine days, Bess entertained her dinner guests to the 'banquet' or sweetmeat course. Much later it was used for surreptitious smoking breaks by musicians entertaining the 6th Duke and his guests.

The East Court

The long view from this quiet garden draws the eye down the half-mile length of the lime tree avenue, planted in 1926. The border of the East Court forms the rim of the 'wineglass', whose stem is the double row of trees. This planting was conceived by Duchess Evelyn who cared deeply for Hardwick's trees.

The central pool is not only decorative – its shape echoing that of the plasterwork on the Long Gallery ceiling – but also functional. It serves as a water supply in case of fire. It was constructed in 1913, during Duchess Evelyn's time at Hardwick. She felt that a pool would be 'nicer than an enclosed tank, but it is very dangerous, being over 11ft deep'. Luckily it wasn't called into use before an inspection by the fire brigade in 1931. The Chesterfield firemen approved the water supply, but pointed out that their fire engine, which weighed five-and-a-half tons, would sink into the soft ground, long before reaching the pond. So a hard path, hidden beneath the turf, was built from the north gateway.

Four yew trees and beds of scented shrub roses underplanted with early and late-flowering perennials, lilies and other late-summer and autumn bulbs add to the peaceful nature of this garden, which is separated from the parkland by a ha-ha dug in 1930, at about the same time that the few remaining deer in the Park were removed.

The North Court

Although this area, until recently the visitors' car park, has traditionally been known as the 'North Orchard' there is no evidence of fruit trees having been planted here. It has proved a useful space from the early 17th century as a coal yard, a timber store, a pheasantry and a paddock for cattle.

The coal yard stored coal mined in the park and its layout was designed so that it 'may bee always kept shutt except when the porter opens it, to deliver out coales for servants chambers and offices, and so keep beggars out of the kitchen'.

Left The central pool in the East Court was created as a water supply in case of fire

Hardwick gardeners
Today's gardening team manages the 7 hectares (18 acres) with the help of volunteers. They not only tend the garden but also produce fruit and vegetables for the restaurant, and run the nursery, propagating plants for the gardens and for sale to visitors. Hardwick holds the National Collection of Eucomis (Pineapple Lily), some of which can be seen in the gardens.

The Parkland and Estate

When Bess built her two great houses high on an escarpment overlooking the Derbyshire countryside, one bearing her initials blazing from the rooftop, she wanted not only to be seen, but also to see.

She could climb to the top of her new house and, from those enormous windows, take in the acres spread before her – knowing that she owned most of it. The view was not all green and pleasant. Bess owned coal mines, iron smelting works, brickworks, quarries and lead mines. They were not all in the immediate environs of the house and were screened by trees, but their chimneys belched out smoke. Today the mines, which increased in number over the centuries, have vanished, although the original quarries from which the Hardwick sandstone was cut can still be seen. Apart from the motorway that cuts through the western edge of the parkland, rural peace surrounds Hardwick and its 7,006-hectare (17,315-acre) estate.

A working estate

Throughout the 17th and 18th centuries Hardwick continued to be a working estate, although the house was occupied only sporadically. Estate accounts show regular work that included repairs to ponds, roads and fence paling, gelding fawns, killing and 'carrying out' venison in the winter, 'browsing' wood for the deer, thatching haystacks, cutting cordwood, killing vermin and 'ravenous fowl' in the park. And so the seasons rolled on, with income from the sale of venison and wood from the thousands of trees.

A dear walk of great perfection

During this time one major project was undertaken by two more Hardwick women. The elderly Countess Spencer and her granddaughter, Harriet, sister to the 6th Duke, worked together in 1797 to mark out the path of what is now called 'Lady Spencer's Walk' through the park. Later Countess Spencer's daughter, the unhappy Georgiana, Duchess of Devonshire, wrote to thank her mother: 'I would not write yesterday not only from being over tir'd but because I could not bear to write till I had seen your dear walk. It is in great perfection.'

'A very goodly prospect'

William Camden described the property in *Britannia*, 1610: 'Higher yet in the very East frontier of this county, upon a rough and a craggie soile standeth Hardwic, which gave name to a family in which possessed the same: out of which descended Lady Elizabeth, Countess of Shrewsbury, who beganne to build there two goodly houses joining in a maner one to the other, which by reason of their lofty situation shew themselves, a farre off to be seene, and yeeld a very goodly prospect.'

Opposite The view from Hardwick Hall towards the old stable buildings

Improving the prospect

Major changes were made for aesthetic reasons in the first half of the 19th century, when the 6th 'Bachelor' Duke inherited.

He re-routed coach drives through the Park, so that views of both the house and its surroundings were improved, and undertook a substantial tree-planting programme. This included the 'platoons', avenues of oaks clustered along the new drives leading to Rowthorne Gate and Blingsby Gate. The trees, planted in small clumps, resemble small troops of soldiers. Rowthorne Lodge, now a luxury holiday cottage, was built at this time.

Water on tap

The second half of the century, following the death of the Bachelor Duke, saw modernisation arrive at Hardwick with the installation, by Thomas Crump of Derby, of a steam engine to pump water to the house. The engine house (its chimney, although detached, still standing), is now home to the Stone Centre adjoining the mason's yard, which was also upgraded in this period. Today's visitors may learn more about the work of Hardwick's master masons here. A flurry of improvements saw a new servants' wing on the north of Hardwick Hall, an overhaul of the stables and other working buildings, including a sawmill, lime house and mess room for workmen. The Great Ponds near the south gate were drained and cleaned. This operation, in 1860, destroyed the marshes where wildfowl bred, so a 'duck decoy' was built nearby.

Below The Stone Centre

Above The gateway to the Stableyard

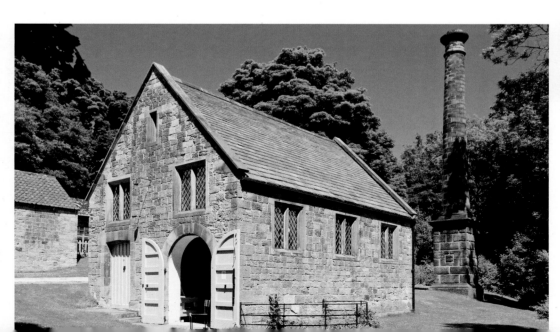

Hardwick's war effort

Two world wars took their toll. The gardens were neglected, deer removed from the park and grassland ploughed. Nevertheless the 'wineglass' lime avenue was planted between the wars and remains a valuable feature. Families were evacuated to Hardwick during the Second World War and parts of the park were used by the RAF and the army. The 1st Parachute Brigade was formed here in 1940 and the School of Airborne Forces, which trained service personnel for the Normandy invasion, established. Links between Hardwick and the Parachute Brigade are still maintained today.

Right The Parachute Brigade practising an exit at Hardwick (1940s)

Stolen bikes' watery grave
Families evacuated to Hardwick during the war were housed in the butler's quarters and housemaids' room, while the steward's room became a dormitory for children. More than 600 bicycles came to light in the silt at the bottom of Millers Pond when it was drained in the 1970s. They had been thrown in by troops who had 'commandeered' them as late night transport after leave in nearby towns.

The estate today

Hardwick Hall, its park and woodland, came to the National Trust in 1959. The Trust then began a process (completed in 2005) of returning the park from arable and dairy farming to grazing by rare breeds. These animals, owned by a tenant farmer, include Longhorn cattle and white-faced woodland sheep, both historic local introductions.

The estate is looked after by a team of rangers and volunteers. Under their care comes the scattering of tenanted farms on the wider estate, the parkland with its footpaths and bridleways, and the stew ponds, which would have provided fish for the house. The team is also responsible for the thousands of trees, using seed from existing stock to grow replacements. Also on the estate is Stainsby Mill (see panel) which, repaired to working order by the Trust, is fed with water from Stainsby Pond and Miller's Pond within the Park.

Ancient woodland

Dovedale Wood, ancient woodland to the south of Hardwick Hall, is home to the rare deadwood beetle (*Corticeus unicolor*) and has SSSI (Site of Special Scientific Interest) status as one of the finest ash and wych-elm woods in the county. Other wildlife habitats abound and the Trust has installed roosts for the thriving populations of bats, including pipistrelle and brown long-eared bats.

Top Stainsby Mill, a restored, water-powered flour mill on the estate

Above View across the Great Pond towards Hardwick Hall (left) and Hardwick Old Hall (right)

An unbroken tradition

An important feature of the estate and an uninterrupted link with the past is the stonemasons' yard, where Hardwick's team of masons works in virtually the same way as their forebears did all those years ago. Sandstone has been quarried from the estate for centuries by the stonemasons who cut and shape, working on platforms known as 'bankers'. The tools they use differ little from those belonging to the master craftsmen who built Hardwick Hall. Today's team repairs damaged stone, not only at Hardwick but also at other National Trust properties.

The functional nature of the estate, managed as part of the ancient landscape, is confirmed by the buildings in the Stableyard. The western range, now largely residential but retaining many original features, once included stables, a brew house and lodgings. Those to the south, once stables, cart sheds and tack rooms now house the restaurant and shop.

A working mill

Stainsby Mill, standing on the site of its 13th-century predecessor, was included in Bess's purchase of the manor of Stainsby in 1593. Totally rebuilt with new machinery in 1850, it has since been repaired by the National Trust and opened to visitors who may buy the flour that they see milled there.

The National Trust at Hardwick

Hardwick Hall is one of England's most perfect Elizabethan houses. Many other great Tudor mansions, built by courtiers to impress their sovereign and their peers, have survived for four centuries. Few have changed so little.

Everything about this magnificent house is unforgettable, exactly as Bess of Hardwick intended. The symmetry of its imposing facade, its height, rising incrementally through three storeys and the six crowning turrets proclaiming her name and status in carefully carved sandstone, remain indelibly in the mind. Nor can anyone forget those windows, thousands of panes of glittering glass, filling the walls with light.

Elizabethan credentials intact

The perfection of the building is matched by its contents. The tapestries, hangings, embroideries, needlework, table-carpets, some furniture and painted friezes are largely those that decorated the house when Bess lived here. Some pieces, contemporaneous with Hardwick, were brought from Chatsworth by her descendants. The 6th Duke in particular moved furniture, paintings and wall hangings to Hardwick. Chatsworth became the main residence of the Cavendish family, the Dukes of Devonshire, while Hardwick, their occasional or holiday home, remained unspoilt and unchanged, its Elizabethan credentials intact.

A huge responsibility

When the National Trust became the caretaker of this unique property over fifty years ago, it faced the huge task of conserving the house and its precious contents, worn by the years and by pollution from the coal mines that once surrounded Hardwick. Not only the exterior stonework, but also interior panelling, flooring and furnishings were affected. The acidity in the dirty air had eaten into the sandstone, allowing water to leak in through eroded window surrounds, while strong sunlight damaged ancient fabrics.

Right A conservator working on the canopy in the Long Gallery

The Trust marshalled its stonemasons who set to work repairing the window mullions and transoms. The stone, cut from the quarries used by the Elizabethan masons, is not hard to match, while the diamond-paned Elizabethan glass with its greenish tinge and tiny air bubbles, was removed until the window frame was secure.

Recreating the ravages of time

Interior conservation is never-ending. Piece by piece the priceless hangings are painstakingly treated and put back on display, although it is impossible to show the original vibrant colours that have become dulled over the centuries. Meanwhile, the Outdoors team have repaired and replanted, defining footpaths and bridleways. Proper care of the trees and ponds and the introduction of new regimes of cattle management has restored the land to good heart.

Visitors, more than 200,000 of them, flock to Hardwick every year, drawn by the promise of England's greatest prodigy house. None can fail to be stirred by its extraordinary architecture, its priceless contents and its dramatic hilltop setting surrounded by beautiful gardens and parkland.

Above Conservation work on the Gideon tapestries

Left Visitors at Hardwick

Bess's Legacy

Bess's story begins and ends at Hardwick where, as a girl, she roamed the hillsides and the pastures with her siblings and half-sisters, playing with wooden toys, enjoying games of hide-and-seek and chanting nursery rhymes.

She learnt her letters and arithmetic from her mother, reading from a 'hornbook' (paper protected by thin translucent horn). She could play a keyboard instrument and was taught to carry herself well and express herself confidently. As she grew she would have helped her mother manage the household.

A lesson well learned

Early financial difficulty taught her that she must take her chances where she could and that the world owed her nothing. She was popular and personable, forming friendships easily. She was also ambitious, determined that the hardships of her youth should never be inflicted on her own children and step-children.

Bess the builder

Marriage brought her wealth and great houses. She honed her architectural skills on Chatsworth, her first building project. Other family houses included Bolsover, Welbeck, Sheffield, Tutbury and Worksop. Her dynastic ambitions were realised through her children, with the dukedoms of Devonshire, Norfolk, Portland, Newcastle and Kingston. Bess, the matriach, fought her way to the top of Elizabethan England.

Left No visitor can ever forget Bess's initials carved against the sky